21ST
CENTURY
DEBATES

NEW RELIGIOUS MOVEMENTS

THE IMPACT ON OUR LIVES

CLAIRE MASON

Raintree
Chicago, Illinois

21st Century Debates Series

Genetics • Surveillance • Internet • Media • Artificial Intelligence • Climate Change • Energy • Rain Forests • Waste, Recycling, and Reuse • Endangered Species • Air Pollution • An Overcrowded World? • Food Supply • Water Supply • World Health • Drugs • Terrorism • Racism • New Religious Movements • Violence in Society • Tourism • Transportation and the Environment

Copyright Permissions
Raintree
100 N. LaSalle, Ste. 1200
Chicago, IL 60602

Published by Raintree, a division of Reed Elsevier, Inc.

Library of Congress Cataloging-in-Publication Data

Mason, Claire.
  New religious movements / Claire Mason.
     v. cm. -- (21st century debates)
Includes bibliographical references and index.
Contents: Cults, sects, or new religions? -- New religious movements around the world -- Controversial new religious movements -- Who joins new religious movements? -- Voluntary conversion or brainwashing? -- Life in a new religious movement -- Leaving new religious movements -- Anticult and countercult movements -- The future : protection, persecution, or tolerance?
  ISBN 0-7398-6032-1
  1. Cults--Juvenile literature. 2. Sects--Juvenile literature. [1. Cults. 2. Sects.] I. Title. II. Series.

  BP603 .M29 2003
  291.9--dc21

                              2002155352

Printed in Hong Kong. Bound in the United States.
1 2 3 4 5 6 7 8 9 LB 07 06 05 04 03

Picture credits: Associated Press 39; Camera Press 9 (Alan Whicker), 11 (Karsh of Ottawa); Corbis 8 (Sankei Shimbun), 12 (Phil Schermeister), 18 and cover foreground (Vince Streano), 25 (Woo David), 28, 46, 48 (Jean Pierre Laffont), 49; Angela Hampton Family Life Picture Library 50 (Angela Hampton); HWPL 53; Impact 4 (Mark Cator), 13 (Alex Macnaughton), 19 (Ben Edwards), 37 (David Reed); Pictorial Press 27, 33, 56; Popperfoto 16 (Kevin Lamarque), 23, 31, 40, 45 (Paulo Whitaker), 47 (Kamal Kishore), 59; Rex Features 14, 15, 26 and cover background; Topham 7 (Toni Michaels/The Image Works), 10, 17, 20 (Larry Kolvoord), 24, 30, 32, 35, 42 (Andrew Lichtenstein), 54.

Cover: foreground picture shows a Hare Krishna devotee in San Francisco; background picture shows 40,000 Moonie couples being married by Reverend Moon in Seoul, Korea, in 1999.

CONTENTS

CULTS, SECTS, OR NEW RELIGIONS?

The birth of new religious movements

Since the dawn of civilization, human beings have held a wide variety of spiritual beliefs, from faith in a single all-powerful god to the worship of nature spirits, such as gods of trees, rivers, and thunder. These beliefs have enriched people's lives but have often led to conflict. This book examines the new religious movements (NRMs) that have emerged, mainly in the developed world since World War II, and the problems they have raised for

A Summer Solstice celebration is held at Stonehenge in Wiltshire, southwest England. This ancient monument is thought to have been used for sacred rituals since around 2000 B.C.E.

governments, individuals, and society as a whole. How can we balance the human right to religious freedom with the state's duty to protect its citizens? What happens when an individual's decision to join a religious movement creates conflict in his or her family?

What is a cult?

NRMs are often described as sects or cults, even though these words have somewhat different meanings. Today the word "cult" is frequently used to discredit new religious movements, particularly in media reports. A cult is, in fact, simply a belief system that focuses on a particular person or place. In a nonreligious context, popular figures, such as Eva Peron of Argentina ("Evita"), Elvis Presley, and the Beatles are often said to have "a cult following." The word "cult" can also be used to refer to something that is very popular among a specialist audience, such as the film *The Rocky Horror Picture Show*.

What is a sect?

Mainstream religions, such as Christianity, Judaism, and Islam, have often given birth to splinter groups. These breakaway groups, known as sects, may change the emphasis of the original religion's teaching, or follow different rules of dress or behavior. The word "sect" implies a troublesome, intense group, as opposed to an established, respectable, mainstream church. Many parent religions disapprove of their related sects, seeing some of them as more extreme than others. For instance, the Salvation Army is considered more acceptable by most Christians than the Unification Church. Some of these movements would object to being called sects. For example, groups as diverse as the Seventh-Day Adventist Church and the Mormons have large numbers of members and would strongly oppose being classified as minor sects.

VIEWPOINT

"If you believe in it, it's a religion or perhaps *the* religion. If you don't care one way or another about it, it's a sect. But if you fear and hate it, it's a cult."
Leo Pfeffer, lawyer and champion of religious freedom

DEBATE

Is there a difference between a cult and a "real" religion? Is one person's religious belief more valid than another's? Who decides?

FACT

Being defined as a religion may enable a movement to claim tax exemption (freedom from tax) in some countries, but it may also mean that it is not allowed to be taught in schools. Scientology fought successfully to be recognized as a religion, thereby gaining tax exemption in the United States.

What are new religious movements?

The current wave of NRMs includes not only sects rooted in Judaism and Christianity, but also movements inspired by Eastern spirituality, paganism, psychology, and even science fiction. Many people prefer to call these "new" or "alternative" religious movements. However, they are not always "new," since they are often rooted in ancient traditions. They are not always "alternative," either. For instance, it is not unusual to be a Mormon if you live in Salt Lake City. Some movements, such as those based on psychology and self-improvement, may not be religions at all.

Counting NRMs

We have touched on the problem of defining a new religious movement. Some definitions refer to belief in a god, which might exclude some of the self-help movements and even Buddhism, while broader definitions might include political ideologies such as Marxism. Counting NRMs depends on the definition used. Excluding political and self-development movements, it is estimated that there are currently fifteen hundred to two thousand NRMs in North America, five hundred in Great Britain, and more than ten thousand new religions among the tribal peoples of the Americas, Asia, Africa, and the Pacific. The United States, Japan, Canada, Britain, West Germany, France, and the Netherlands, where mainstream religion is in decline, have been fruitful sites for many NRMs. In contrast, regions where mainstream religions are strong, such as Italy, Greece, Spain, Ireland, and Austria, have seen very little NRM activity.

There is no indication that any NRMs will become major religions and, despite the controversy surrounding them, these movements have only affected the lives of a tiny fraction of the population of any country. The exception is Japan, where there are up to forty thousand emerging religions and between 10 and 20 percent of the population has been associated with an NRM.

Counting NRM members also presents problems, since it is difficult to define what constitutes membership. In addition, many people, such as Freemasons, choose to keep their membership secret. Only a relatively small number of people live in an NRM center or work full-time for a movement. But far larger numbers meditate each day or attend a weekly yoga or tai chi class; should they be defined as NRM members?

DEBATE

Should NRMs be officially recognized and given the same (tax exempt) charitable status as mainstream religions?

A woman meditates before her morning jog in Chicago.

VIEWPOINT

"Some members of some religious movements commit crimes; the organizational structure of some religious movements opens the way for abuses of authority. But criminal, dangerous, or antisocial behavior is by no means typical of all religious movements. Simply because a religion is unfamiliar, new, or 'different' does not mean that it is necessarily a cause for concern."

Information Network Focus on Religious Movements (INFORM), an organization that aims to provide objective information about NRMs

Defining a cult

Do NRMs have no more in common than that someone has labeled them as NRMs or cults? The Cult Information Centre (CIC) in Britain, which sees these movements as "a threat to the well-being of the individual and the family," defines a cult as having the following characteristics:

1) It uses psychological coercion to recruit, indoctrinate, and retain its members. (This means that the group apparently uses some form of mind control or powerful persuasion to "brainwash" people into accepting its beliefs without question.)
2) It forms an elitist totalitarian society. (This means that the group forms a closed society, where everything is controlled by the leader or his or her deputies. Its members believe they are superior or "chosen" by a god and are an exclusive community of "the saved.")

Shoko Asahara, former leader of Aum Shinrikyo, a controversial Japanese sect that carried out a toxic gas attack on the Tokyo Underground in 1995, was seen as a messianic figure by his followers.

3) Its founder/leader is self-appointed, dogmatic, messianic, not accountable, and has charisma. (This means that the group's members believe that the leader possesses a very special, possibly divine, quality. As a consequence, the followers are willing to grant their leader a special kind of authority over them.)

4) It believes "the end justifies the means" in order to raise funds or recruit people. (This means that the group will use any methods, legal or illegal, to raise money or increase their membership.)

5) Its wealth is not used to benefit its members or society as a whole.

Many NRMs live in communities isolated from the rest of society, with their own schools and childcare arrangements.

This negative picture of NRMs is based on the groups that have attracted the most notoriety. The perception that NRMs are dangerous is supported by high-profile incidents reported in the media involving so-called "evil cults," "killer cults," and "suicide cults."

However, as we will see, NRMs are extremely diverse, with differing origins, beliefs, and practices. The controversial groups described in pages 28 to 33 are by no means representative of all new religious movements. Indeed, groups in favor of religious tolerance argue that the so-called characteristics of cults (listed above) have been exaggerated, and the fact that many NRM followers strive to lead moral and spiritual lives has been largely ignored.

NEW RELIGIOUS MOVEMENTS AROUND THE WORLD

Three of the Beatles, (left to right) Paul McCartney, George Harrison, and John Lennon, listen to their guru, the Maharishi Mahesh Yogi. The Maharishi brought Transcendental Meditation (TM) into the limelight when he taught the Beatles how to meditate in 1968. Their adoption of TM was widely publicized.

The rise of new religious movements
During the 20th century, fewer people in developed countries belonged to a mainstream religion, and the pursuit of wealth became more important. As a reaction to this growing materialism, many people started to search for greater meaning in life and many found this in new religions. This resulted in a dramatic increase in NRMs, a rise that reached its height in the 1960s and 1970s. While earlier NRMs, such as Jehovah's Witnesses and the Salvation Army, could be recognized as sects within the Judeo-Christian tradition, the new NRMs, such as the International Society for Krishna Consciousness (ISKCON) and Transcendental Meditation (TM), came from a wide range of traditions, many of them alien to the developed world until fairly recently.

In 1965 the United States encouraged Asian immigration, partly to gain Asian support for the war in Vietnam. Suddenly hundreds of thousands of Asian people arrived in the United States, together with Asian religious missionaries. This access to Eastern spirituality coincided with the rise of youth culture (the first time that young people's interests in music, art, and alternative lifestyles had an influence on mainstream society). Areas such as California, New York, Oregon, and Washington became fertile ground for a new generation of religious movements as diverse as ISKCON and the Children of God. These movements were soon to spread throughout the developed world.

There was also a rapid rise in the popularity of Islam among black peoples. This trend began in the United States in the 1930s with the formation of the African-American Nation of Islam, which combined religion with a political movement for social empowerment.

Islamic sectarian movements have caused concern in both Islamic and non-Islamic states. For instance, in 2001 terrorists assumed to be backed by the Taliban regime in Afghanistan destroyed the entire World Trade Center in New York, killing thousands.

From the 1960s onward, interest in science and psychology, particularly in the United States, gave rise to a whole range of professional "self-development" and "therapy" movements. In 1973 Werner Erhard, a former used-car and encyclopedia salesman, founded Erhard Seminars Training (EST), or "est," which aims to "empower" people to "transform" their lives, better their relationships, and improve their communication skills.

Werner Erhard was the founder of EST. Now known as The Forum, EST was one of the first self-development movements.

FACT

According to Gordon Melton, director of the Institute for the Study of American Religion, California has earned the name "Cultifornia" for two reasons. First, the spread of unconventional religions mainly occurs in towns and cities, and California is the only state with three major urban centers (Los Angeles, San Francisco, and San Diego). Secondly, many NRMs were imported from Asia, so the West Coast is their logical starting point.

Christian sects

Christian sects usually differ from conventional Christian groups in two main ways. First of all, they interpret the Bible differently from other groups, or give a particular aspect of the Bible more emphasis than mainstream churches do. For instance, Jehovah's Witnesses focus on the importance of door-to-door visits and distributing their literature.

Second, these Christian sects often have an "extrascriptural" source of authority that is given the same weight as the Bible. Sometimes known as a "bible in the left hand," this source of teaching focuses on the sect's particular beliefs. For example, the Church of Jesus Christ of Latter-Day Saints, usually known as the Mormon religion, has the Book of Mormon. According to Mormon history, this text was translated from golden plates unearthed by the church's founder, Joseph Smith, following his vision of the angel Morani in 1823.

The Mormon Tabernacle Choir performs in Salt Lake City, Utah, in 1988.

The enthusiasm of some of these sectarian groups can lead to disagreements with more conservative Christian churches. For example, some extreme Christian sects believe that members of their group have a particular part to play at the end of the world (the apocalypse). This belief became particularly prominent in the years leading up to the millennium. Some of these groups associated the dawning of a new millennium with the second coming of the Messiah (the first coming being that of Jesus) and the end of the world.

There are a great many Christian sects, ranging from well-established movements such as the Jehovah's Witnesses, the Salvation Army, and the Seventh-Day Adventist Church, to new movements such as the Unification Church, the Family (formerly called the Children of God), the Branch Davidians, the Eternal Flame Foundation, and the Jesus Fellowship Church, or Jesus Army. These movements vary a great deal in their beliefs and practices, from the Jesus Army with its slogan "Love, Power, and Sacrifice" and the promise of its combat-clad members to "fight for YOU," to the Eternal Flame Foundation, whose members believe they have achieved physical immortality.

FACT

According to a survey conducted in 1999, 72 percent of Americans believed that the world would come to a sudden end one day. Of these, 15 percent thought that this was likely to coincide with the millennium.

Jesus Army members perform a baptism in Trafalgar Square fountain, London.

The Unification Church

The Unification Church is perhaps the best known of the new wave of religious movements. It is led

The Reverend Sun Myung Moon is founder and leader of the Unification Church.

by the Reverend Sun Myung Moon, who was born in 1920 in what is now North Korea. He founded the Holy Spirit Association for the Unification of World Christianity in South Korea in 1954.

Members are popularly known as "Moonies," a name that followers dislike because of its association with bad publicity. Now officially known as the Family Federation for World Peace and Unification, the movement's basic beliefs are contained in a book called the *Divine Principle*. This book offers a reinterpretation of the Old and New Testaments, combined with some elements of Eastern philosophy and further revelations from Reverend Moon, whom his followers believe to be the Messiah.

The movement became prominent in the developed world in the early 1970s when Moon moved to the United States and began organizing large rallies and speaking tours. Members were often college age, well educated, and from middle-class backgrounds. The Unification Church is particularly famous for its mass weddings. In the interest of world unification, Moon often selects partners of different nationalities. Candidates assemble in a hall and are matched up by Moon. Two thousand or more couples can be married in one ceremony.

VIEWPOINTS

"However passionate Moon's followers may be, British families have been destroyed by the Moonies: losing their children, both emotionally and physically, to a cult which in reality is a vast, powerful, and well-organized multi-million-pound corporation."
The Mail on Sunday *[the* Daily Mail *newspaper led a campaign against the Unification Church in Britain]*

"The history of misrepresentation of new or unpopular religions is long and curious. In the light of the...Daily Mail campaign against the Unification Church, we see again the type of stereotyping which was very useful to the Nazis in their elimination of the Jews. Ironically it is not the 'Moonies' who are 'brainwashed' but it is the public...."
The Unification Church

Reverend Moon and his wife regularly conduct mass weddings involving thousands of couples. However, the weddings are not legally recognized, obliging the couples to have a civil ceremony afterward.

FACT

Immigration officials in the United States, Great Britain, and former West Germany have tried to exclude the Reverend Moon from their countries to prevent missionary rallies. For instance, in 1995 then–British Home Secretary Michael Howard ordered that Moon be excluded on the grounds that his presence was "not conducive to the public good." The British High Court later ruled that Howard had acted unlawfully.

In the 1970s Moonies sold flowers, clothes, plants, candy, and candles from door to door. Today, members are more likely to work in a business owned by the Unification Church. These include newspapers (such as *The Washington Times*), television stations, hotel chains, universities, factories, real estate businesses, and even a ballet company. In February 2000 the Unification Church claimed to have 4.5 million members worldwide, with the largest branches in Nigeria, the Philippines, Brazil, South Korea, and Japan.

Moon has been criticized for his vast personal fortune and extravagant lifestyle. The Unification Church has also been accused by its opponents of evading taxes, subjecting its members to poor living conditions, and supporting extreme right-wing politicians, including nationalist French politician Jean-Marie Le Pen and Chilean politician Augusto Pinochet.

DEBATE

Should Unification Church representatives be prevented from entering countries to preach? What about freedom of speech and freedom of belief?

Eastern-inspired NRMs

NRMs of Eastern origin tend to share certain beliefs. For example, most of them believe that we exist on a physical, mental, and spiritual level, and that enlightenment involves achieving a sense of oneness with the universe. Christians ask God to grant salvation, whereas devotees of most Eastern NRMs search for spiritual perfection within themselves. Instead of a priest, devotees often have a guru or teacher, a charismatic leader sometimes thought to be an embodiment of God. There may be an emphasis on discipline, meditation, giving up material wealth, and seeking inner peace.

As one of the world's oldest religious, spiritual, and philosophical traditions, Hinduism has inspired a huge number of movements. The best known of these include ISKCON, or the International Society for Krishna Consciousness (also known as Hare Krishna), Brahma Kumaris (also known as Raja Yoga), Ananda Marga (or Tantric Yoga), Rajneeshism (also referred to as Osho International, the Sannyasins, or the Orange People), and Elan Vital (also called the Divine Light Mission). Transcendental Meditation appears under several names, including TM, Yogic Flying, and the Maharishi Foundation. Like many Eastern practices, such as yoga and tai chi, Transcendental Meditation is often taught as a relaxation technique separate from its Hindu origins. There are also various new Buddhist sects, including Zen and

At the 1997 general election in London, members of the Natural Law Party demonstrated Yogic Flying (a kind of meditation in which practitioners appear to levitate by bouncing) in order to encourage voters to opt for "conflict-free politics and a state of bubbling bliss."

Nichiren Shoshu Buddhism. While the unique nature of these movements often draws suspicion from both traditional religious and secular sides in developed countries, tens of thousands of people who are associated with movements such as ISKCON are of Asian origin to begin with.

The Hindu god Vishnu is worshiped particularly in his eighth reincarnation as the handsome Krishna who inspired passionate desires through the sweet music of his flute.

ISKCON

The International Society for Krishna Consciousness, otherwise known as the Hare Krishna movement, is one of the most visible NRMs. Founded by Calcutta-born A. C. Bhaktivedanta Swami Prabhupada (1896–1977) in the United States in 1966, the movement has its roots in Vaishnava Hinduism, a 16th-century development of the Hindu tradition that takes the Bhagavad-Gita as its central scripture. In this sense, Krishna Consciousness is not a new religious movement—it is a modern version of an old tradition, directed mainly at people in the Western (developed) world rather than in the East.

FACT

The late former Beatle George Harrison helped in the recording of ISKCON's song "Hare Krishna Mantra" in 1968. Harrison donated a mansion in Hertfordshire, England, to the movement. This is still the British headquarters of ISKCON.

In 1965 Prabhupada went to the United States, where he quickly gained a following in the Bowery district of New York City and in the Haight-Ashbury district of San Francisco. ISKCON spread rapidly in the United States and Britain, initially attracting former hippies and drug-users, many of whom were drawn to the sense of identity and the simple lifestyle offered by the movement.

ISKCON devotees believe that they can find perfect happiness by living a life of deep spirituality. To achieve this, they chant their Hare Krishna mantra 1,728 times a day, counting 16 rounds of 108 beads (worn as a necklace) first thing in the morning. This takes about two hours. Members living in a community, or ashram, which was very popular in the 1970s, rise at 4:00 A.M. for worship.

Although this movement has caused some controversy, many members of the Hindu community in the West and in India accept ISKCON as a genuine Hindu sect. All ISKCON members have to give up meat, fish, eggs, alcohol, tobacco, drugs, tea, coffee, gambling, sports, games, novels, and sex (except for procreation within

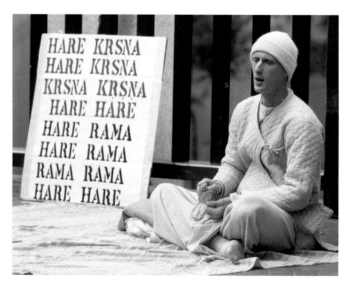

A Hare Krishna devotee sits on a blanket and chants in San Francisco in the early 1980s.

marriage). The devotees' most important task is *sankirtan* (distributing Krishna literature, collecting donations, and recruiting new members). ISKCON members often have shaved heads and pigtails and dress in saffron (orange) robes.

A Hare Krishna group holds an open-air picnic celebration.

The movement has many charitable programs, including Hare Krishna Food for Life, which distributes free meals to the needy. However, ISKCON has also been criticized for putting the duties of worship before the welfare of followers' children. In 2000 a number of former members sued ISKCON, alleging that extensive child abuse had taken place at ISKCON boarding schools in the 1970s and 1980s. In 2002, twelve of nearly fifty ISKCON temples in the United States filed for bankruptcy protection in response to the 400-million-dollar lawsuit. All ISKCON schools have since shut down.

DEBATE

Should parents be allowed to raise children in any faith they want? What about the welfare of the children? What about the human right to religious freedom?

Self-development movements

Self-development movements are often referred to as "self religions" because they offer to develop the individual's potential. In contrast to Eastern-inspired movements, self-improvement NRMs place great importance on professional and material success. For their followers, man, rather than God, is the center of the universe, and the ultimate goal is to get what you want out of life.

The self-development industry has grown very quickly in recent decades—from bestselling books to training courses teaching various self-improvement techniques. Many of these movements offer courses of "therapy" focusing on personal relationships, success, self-esteem, effectiveness, and communication skills, some of which are used by business organizations and governments. Participants are usually middle-class

A woman browsing in the psychology section of a bookstore. Sales of popular psychology and self-development books have been booming since the 1960s.

professionals who are not expected to stop working while taking courses. In fact, a substantial salary is often required to be able to afford the course fees.

Several of these movements, such as Neuro-Linguistic Programming (NLP), which has achieved great success in the business world, are highly respected. However, some self-development movements have been criticized for not being open enough about their wider belief system. For instance, a person might attend a course on succeeding in the workplace without realizing that the technique being taught was part of a religion. Some of these "self religions" have also been criticized for their refusal to "let go" of people once they have become involved, offering the promise of ever-greater benefits from each new course.

Many of these courses stem from Erhard Seminars Training (EST), the personal development program that generated much controversy in the 1960s due to its verbally abusive style of training. Students would be shouted at by the course leader and subjected to extreme pressure in order to "break down their defenses" and "open them up to success." The EST courses, now known as The Forum, take place over two consecutive weekends and one three-hour evening. There are "graduates" of The Forum who claim that the experience has benefited them a great deal, making them more effective in both their personal and professional lives. However, other people have found the intensity of the seminars extremely disturbing.

Movements such as the Human Potential Movement (which includes Co-Counseling, Gestalt Therapy, and Rebirthing), Insight, and The Emin, tend to use a combination of business or sales techniques and methods employed in psychotherapy.

DEBATE

Are self-development movements just a way of getting money from vulnerable people, or do they offer a genuine means to self-improvement?

VIEWPOINTS

"It is like any new religion. The attacks are uniformly unfounded and sooner or later they fall by the wayside.... If someone is attacking us or trying to harm the church, we will take action. We are not taking a stance for ourselves, we are taking a stance for religious freedom."
Graeme Wilson, Head of Public Affairs, Scientology, Britain

"Scientology is quite likely the most ruthless, the most classically terroristic, the most litigious, and the most lucrative cult the country has ever seen. No cult extracts more money from its members."
Cynthia Kisser, director of the Cult Awareness Network, an anticult movement since purchased by a group including Scientologists

The Church of Scientology

Scientology was founded by Lafayette Ron Hubbard (1911–1986), a writer known for his science-fiction stories. He published *Dianetics: The Modern Science of Mental Health* in 1950. It was extremely popular in therapy-conscious America and is still a bestseller. He founded the Church of Scientology in 1954.

Dianetic therapy is based on the idea that people's minds store a mental image—"Engram"—of each unpleasant thing that happens to them in this life and in past lives. These "Engrams" can be triggered by association and can be a barrier to achieving one's full potential. Scientologists claim that a senior Scientologist, acting as an "Auditor," can get rid of these "Engrams" and help people to become "Clear," or optimum, individuals. Beyond Clear, there are a further 15 levels of enlightenment that are not revealed to more junior devotees.

Scientology is probably the wealthiest and most powerful of the new religious movements. A frequent complaint is the amount of money that Scientologists pay for their courses, sometimes leading people to amass huge debts. Critics say there are a never-ending number of courses, some of them costing up to $78,000 per person.

Scientologists have fought to be classed as a tax-exempt religion and sued those who they believe have misrepresented their aims and activities. They have come into conflict with several organizations in the United States, including the Federal Bureau of Investigation (FBI), the Internal Revenue Service (IRS), and the Food and Drugs Administration (FDA). Many governments, including those of Britain, Germany, and France, have attempted to ban or restrict the operations of the church.

In 1993, after four decades of court battles, the IRS granted Scientology tax exemption as a religious institution. By contrast, in 1999 the British Charity Commission barred Scientology from charitable status, ruling that it failed to promote the "moral and spiritual welfare" of the community.

The church often claims to have eight million members, although this includes people who have only had a few introductory sessions. A figure of 750,000 members is thought to be more realistic. Worldwide, Scientology's income has been put at about $318 million per year. The organization has brought hundreds of lawsuits and pays out an estimated $13 million annually to more than one hundred lawyers.

At a 1997 court hearing in Washington, D.C., actor and Scientologist John Travolta listens as German Scientologist Claudia Engel discusses the religious persecution she believes she has suffered due to the German government's opposition to the Church of Scientology.

FACT

Many people believe in the benefits of Dianetic Therapy, and there are many celebrity Scientologists, including Hollywood actors John Travolta, Kirstie Alley, Sharon Stone, Demi Moore, and Tom Cruise.

DEBATE

Is Scientology a religion or a cult, and is there a difference? Are its followers being helped to live happier, more rewarding lives? Or are they being exploited? Is the organization a victim of persecution, or does it victimize its members?

FACT

The French founder of the 40,000-member Raëlian movement, former race-car driver and journalist Claude Vorilhon, has offered funding and volunteers to help an American scientist to realize his dream of cloning humans. The Raëlians believe that life on earth was created scientifically by visiting extraterrestrials called the Elohim, and that humanity's survival depends on cloning.

New Age NRMs

New Age and neopagan movements, such as Wicca (see pp. 26–27) and Druidism, are often based on belief in many gods or nature spirits, as worshiped in ancient pre-Christian religions. Followers of these NRMs wish to live in harmony with nature, and they may perform rituals to celebrate their relationship with the cosmos. Many New Age movements draw on ancient traditions, including alchemy, paganism, Druidism, cabalism, and voodoo, as well as Egyptian, Chinese, Greek, Roman, Celtic, and Norse mythology. They are also associated with a wide range of alternative therapies, from Alexander Technique and aromatherapy to homeopathy and acupuncture.

Other New Age movements also look back to secret ancient traditions. By the 1600s various Rosicrucian orders were based on rediscovered Christian, Egyptian, and Greek mystic texts. In the 1800s Madame Helena Blavatsky developed a system called theosophy to study ancient religions, philosophies, and sciences. Several of these movements believe in "Secret Masters" who they say have guarded the "Truth," the origin of all world religions, for thousands of years.

There are also New Age movements that are inspired by

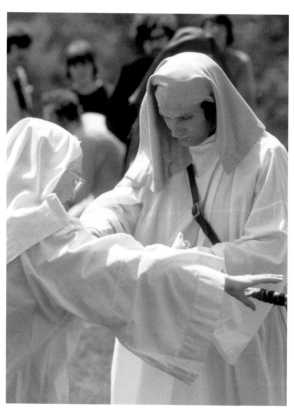

Druids celebrate the spring fire festival of Beltaine at Glastonbury Tor, in southwest England, a place that they believe to be full of cosmic energy.

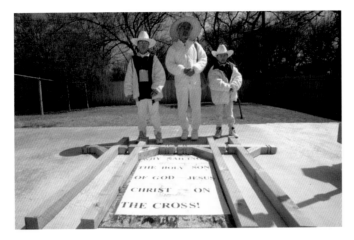

Members of a Taiwanese "flying saucer cult" wait at a site in Texas for God to descend from space.

science fiction or by new developments in science and technology, such as the International Fortean Society, the Society for the Investigation of the Unexplained, the Raëlians, and other so-called "flying saucer cults."

Satanism

Most New Age movements are fairly uncontroversial. However, satanism has always attracted opposition, particularly from Christian organizations, because its followers worship Satan (or the devil) rather than God. The most notorious British satanist, Aleister Crowley (1875–1947), was a mystic who enjoyed experimenting with drugs and sex and became known as "the wickedest man alive." In 1966 Anton LaVey founded the Church of Satan in San Francisco and wrote *The Satanic Bible*.

More recently, satanism has made headlines through its association with musicians such as the band Marilyn Manson and from the wave of "satanic ritual abuse" (SRA) allegations against satanists and Wiccans in the 1990s. Following police and government investigations in numerous countries, it was concluded that SRA was largely a myth. Nevertheless the negative image of satanists persists in the media.

VIEWPOINTS

"More than ever, we need a spirituality that is rooted in a love of nature, a love of the land."
Member of the Order of Bards, Ovates, and Druids

"I don't believe that magic is supernatural, only that it is supernormal. That it works for reasons that science cannot yet understand."
Anton LaVey, high priest of the Church of Satan

FACT

Tens of thousands of women were murdered during the witch hunts of the 1300s through 1700s for an assortment of "evils," including spinsterhood and warts. In Salem, Massachusetts, in 1692, 19 people accused of witchcraft were hanged. A BBC news story in 1995 reported that over one thousand women had recently been burned to death in South Africa because neighbors had accused them of being witches.

Wicca

The word "witch" comes from the Anglo-Saxon word "wicca," meaning a person—such as a healer, midwife, or fortune teller—skilled in influencing the unseen forces of nature. Wicca, also known as white witchcraft or "the Craft," is the largest and best-known neopagan movement. It is becoming popular in the United States, and is perhaps the fastest-growing religion in Britain. It is estimated that there are about one million witches worldwide. The fastest rise has been among women, who are often attracted to the movement's emphasis on nature and worship of the Goddess (rather than the Christian "male" God).

Wicca draws on a number of traditions, but its modern form is largely the legacy of retired British civil servant Gerald Gardner (1884–1964), who built on the work of British Egyptologist Margaret Murray. He had a lifelong interest in folklore, magic, and mysticism. Gardner joined a coven (a group of witches) in 1939 and recreated witchcraft ceremonies in his book *Witchcraft Today*.

Covens meet regularly to mark seasonal festivals and full moons. Wicca celebrates eight of these festivals: Samhain (also known as Hallowe'en), Winter Solstice, Imbolg (also known as Candlemas), Spring Equinox, Beltaine

A modern-day American white witch, Andrew Jackson, wears the Wicca symbol (a pentagram, or five-pointed star).

British actress Maggie Smith in the movie based on J. K. Rowling's book Harry Potter and the Sorcerer's Stone. Some schools in Kansas and Colorado have banned the Harry Potter books because they are thought to promote witchcraft.

(May Day), Summer Solstice, Lughnasad (Lammas or Harvest Festival), and the Autumn Equinox. They perform magic spells and other rituals, meditations, and creative visualizations (imagining a new reality and trying to make this come true using repetition and willpower). However, the Pagan Federation insists: "Witchcraft is not just about spells; it is a serious, nature-based, mystery religion in which the natural world is seen to be sacred."

Covens are usually led by a priest and priestess, though in most covens the high priestess is in charge of the rituals. In contrast to the fairytale image of witches as old women, they can be both men and women, young and old. Many of them are middle-class professionals with families and mortgages. White magic is used for insight, personal growth, spirituality, and power, rather than for aggression or revenge.

VIEWPOINTS

"Wiccans have little in common with the witch on the broom[stick] eating baby children, although they share the idea of unseen magic and working with unseen powers."
Cynthia Eller, assistant professor of women and religion, Montclair State University, New Jersey

"You can always tell a witch. They have webbed feet and a bald head."
Roald Dahl, The Witches

CONTROVERSIAL NEW RELIGIOUS MOVEMENTS

Why are NRMs controversial?

Media reports often suggest that all NRMs are dangerous and destructive, but this may be in part because negative stories about NRMs tend to make more exciting headlines. In this atmosphere of suspicion, many NRMs are reluctant to speak to the media to defend themselves, believing they will not be given a fair hearing. In the 1970s some anticult movements were established. They stirred up fears of mass youth conversion and portrayed NRM leaders as unscrupulous, power-crazed figures. However, the biggest influence on public attitudes has been a number of high-profile tragedies involving NRMs.

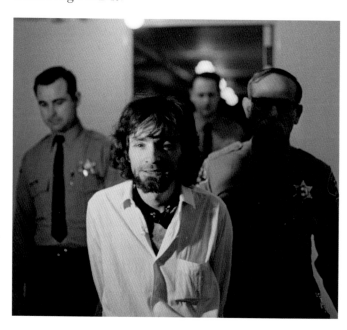

Charles Manson goes to court in January 1971, escorted by police, for the final stage of the Tate-LaBianca trial, in which he and three female members of the "Manson Family" were charged with murder.

These so-called "killer cults" all tend to share apocalyptic beliefs, charismatic leaders, and isolation from society. They often face hostility from the public, leading them to feel that they are at war with the outside world. Although there are thousands of peaceful, positive NRMs across the world, and most of the crimes, murders, and suicides that happen every year have nothing to do with religion, the following tragic incidents demonstrate the dangers of religious extremism and total obedience to a leader. Nevertheless, there is no evidence that members of NRMs are more likely than other people to commit crimes.

Charles Manson—The Tate-LaBianca murders

On August 9, 1969, five people were murdered in a mansion in an exclusive area of Los Angeles. Among those found dead were pregnant actress Sharon Tate (wife of movie director Roman Polanski) and coffee heiress Abigail Folger. The following evening, Rosemary and Leno LaBianca, a wealthy couple, were stabbed to death in their home on the edge of Hollywood.

The police charged the Manson Family, a paramilitary mystic group that showed some cultic tendencies, with the murders. Although their leader, Charles Miles Manson, was not physically present at the crime scenes, a jury convicted him of inciting the murders as part of his vision of a coming apocalypse. While the Manson Family did not share clearly defined religious ideas or practices, Manson exercised authoritarian control over his "slaves," demanding total obedience and forbidding them to ask the question "Why?" Manson's death sentence was changed to life imprisonment and, now in his sixties, he has a new generation of followers who have dedicated numerous websites to him.

VIEWPOINT

"Most of the people at the ranch that you call The Family were just people that you did not want, people that were alongside the road, that their parents had kicked out.... So I did the best I could and I took them up on my garbage dump and I told them this: that in love there is no wrong...."
Charles Manson, trial transcript

FACT

Manson is said to have tested his followers' devotion by holding a knife to their throats and asking if they would let him kill them. When a follower answered yes, Manson would hand the follower the knife and say, "Now you can kill me, too."

VIEWPOINT

VIEWPOINT

"Cults are proliferating.... We know, and we must never forget, that every path leads somewhere. The path of segregation leads to lynching. The path of anti-Semitism leads to Auschwitz. The path of cults leads to Jonestown. We ignore this fact at our peril."
Rabbi Maurice Davis, White Plains, New York, USA

The People's Temple, Jonestown, Guyana

On November 18, 1978, People's Temple leader Jim Jones and 913 of his followers died after drinking a cyanide-laced batch of Kool Aid. Jones had been a Protestant pastor in the United States, but he led his movement to South America, intending to establish a community called Jonestown in which people would live in harmony as equals. However, when Congressman Leo Ryan and several journalists came to investigate allegations that people were being held there against their will, they were shot. Shortly thereafter, the members of Jonestown either poisoned themselves or were also shot. When the story was reported in the media, the People's Temple was labeled a "cult" and came to symbolize all that was bad about new religious movements.

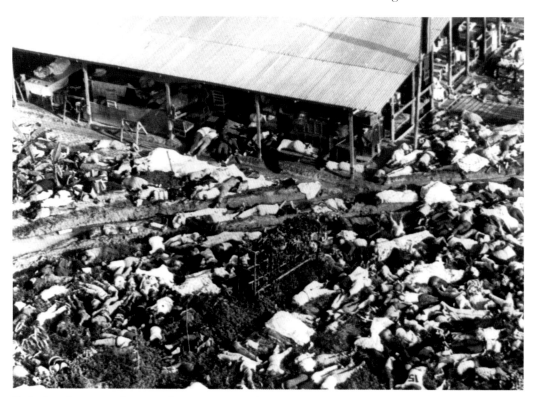

Bodies litter Jonestown, Guyana, where in 1978 more than nine hundred members of the People's Temple died. The Reverend Jim Jones, founder and leader of the cult, died along with his followers.

Branch Davidians

A subsect of the Seventh-Day Adventist Church, the Branch Davidians were based in an isolated community in Waco, Texas. Vernon Howell took over the movement in 1990, changing his name to David Koresh ("David" after the King of Jews, and "Koresh" after God's supposed surname, meaning "death" or "destroyer"). The group's compound was heavily armed, and in 1993 it was raided by the Bureau of Alcohol, Tobacco, and Firearms (ATF). After several raiders were killed, the Branch Davidians were besieged by the FBI for 51 days. Live television crews covered the entire siege. Their reports focused on the idea that although Koresh was a charismatic leader, his mental health was in question.

On April 19, a fire broke out, causing the stockpiled weapons and ammunition to explode. Eighty people died in the fire, including 17 children. There were just nine survivors. The FBI states that members set fire to the compound. Survivors deny this, claiming that the fire was started by the FBI's attack. Although an investigation in 2000 absolved the government of wrondoing, controversy still exists.

The Branch Davidian compound in Waco, Texas, bursts into flames in 1993.

Order of the Solar Temple

More than seventy members of the Order of the Solar Temple died in Canada, France, and Switzerland between 1994 and 1997. They were an apocalyptic group that believed the world would end in 1994. They also believed that their leader, Joseph Di Mambro, had been a member of the Knights Templar during the Crusades (in the Middle Ages) and that he would lead them, through death, to the planet Sirius. By leaving their human bodies, they thought they would receive invisible, "solar" ones. The subsequent murders and suicides among the members appear to have been aimed at realizing this goal.

Aum Shinrikyo

Aum Shinrikyo is usually translated as the "Supreme Truth Society." This Japanese NRM's beliefs were based on a combination of Buddhism, Apocalyptic Christianity, and a focus on the Hindu

Passengers on the Tokyo subway suffer the effects of the Aum Shinrikyo sect's toxic gas attack in 1995.

god of creation and destruction, Shiva. The group came to much public attention following its sarin nerve gas attack on the Tokyo subway in 1995, in which 12 members of the public were killed and thousands were injured. This was the culmination of a series of killings and sparked particular public concern, as Aum Shinrikyo was the first NRM to turn its destructive impulses on society at large. In January 2000 the movement, now known as Aleph, dissociated itself from leader Shoko Asahara and established a new code of conduct to ensure that its two thousand members did not break the law.

Heaven's Gate

Heaven's Gate followers believed they were divine spirits trapped in human shells. They awaited a sign to show that they could move on to their "next level of development." In 1996 leader Marshall Herff Applewhite warned that members who stayed on Earth would surely die. When Comet Hale-Bopp approached Earth in March 1997, one photograph was thought to show a small dot in its wake. Believing this was an alien spacecraft, Heaven's Gate followers thought it had come to collect them. It seems that the members agreed to help one another die. One morning all 39 were found dead in their communal house.

This screen shot shows the Heaven's Gate website. All 39 members of this NRM died in 1997.

DEBATE

Should governments pass laws banning NRMs that they believe to be dangerous?

WHO JOINS NEW RELIGIOUS MOVEMENTS?

Typical NRM converts

One of the reasons for the controversy surrounding NRMs is the fact that their members are often well-educated, middle-class young people with good career prospects. Away from the controlling influence of their parents, students have the time and freedom to give total commitment to such groups. University campuses therefore used to be a fertile recruitment ground for movements including the Unification Church, Children of God (also known as COG, or The Family), and ISKCON. The International Church of Christ has described campuses as "the goose that laid the golden egg," and the Unification Church has a youth recruitment wing, the Collegiate Association for the Research of Principles (CARP). Considerable numbers of young people were recruited to NRMs the 1960s and 1970s, to the alarm of their parents.

Typical converts are young idealists and spiritual seekers, eager to feel that they are doing something to "save the world." As well as spreading their beliefs, NRMs are involved in a number of programs, from environmental protest and drug rehabilitation courses to disaster and famine relief operations. These "youth religions" are often opposed on the grounds that they prevent young people from satisfactorily completing their courses of education and embarking on conventional careers. Self-development movement members tend to be older, usually in their thirties and forties,

Students at the University of Colorado, Boulder, appear to experience religious ecstasy at the Holy Man Jam in 1970.

in part because they need an income to pay for courses, which can run into thousands of dollars.

The young age of many NRM members may account for some of the movements' common characteristics, such as religious enthusiasm, idealism, and unwillingness to compromise their beliefs or lifestyle. While the first generation of recruits to an emerging religion may be in their twenties, the average age of these first recruits increases over time, when new converts join, some members leave, and others grow older. There are now a growing number of children and adults who have been born into NRMs.

Recruits to the better-known NRMs are mainly white, although sects such as the Jehovah's Witnesses and the Black Hebrew Israelites have large numbers of black members. Many of the ill-fated members of the Branch Davidians (see p. 31) and the People's Temple (see p. 30) were people from disadvantaged backgrounds.

DEBATE

What is it about the late 20th and early 21st centuries that has led young people to look to NRMs, while traditional churches are finding it difficult to recruit young people?

VIEWPOINTS

"Push" factors

Traditional Christian churches are finding it difficult to recruit young people, but some NRMs are seen as attractive, perhaps because they are perceived as young, energetic, and vibrant, rather than as dusty, conservative institutions. Most people in developed countries now have all their physical needs satisfied, but may still have unfulfilled spiritual needs. For some people, NRMs can fill this gap in their lives and answer questions such as "Why are we here?" and "What happens after death?"

Despite rising standards of living in developed countries, many people face a loss of job security and a breakdown in traditional family and social structures. For some, the resulting anxiety and stress can be relieved by giving up control of their own lives and handing responsibility to a group, teacher, or leader who claims to have all the answers.

"Pull" factors

Some NRMs offer clear answers to religious questions as well as clear steps to follow to achieve enlightenment. Movements may also give recruits the opportunity to explore philosophical questions and provide access to "ancient truths." Some movements offer members the chance to "save the world" and thus save themselves from a "forthcoming apocalypse."

However, religion is not necessarily the most important aspect of their appeal. Many young people are attracted to the promise of authority and leadership, which can presumably give direction and meaning to their lives. NRMs offer members a family, instant friendship and affection, and a sense of belonging to a community of like-minded people. This is particularly appealing to those who are lonely or unsure about their place in the world, or who are battling drug or alcohol dependency.

Some movements promise improved health and, in the case of the Eternal Flame Foundation, even immortality. It is claimed that many of the rituals practiced by NRMs, such as chanting, prayer, and meditation, have been scientifically proven to be beneficial in reducing stress and improving mental health.

The Findhorn Community, established in northeast Scotland in 1962, offers friendship and a peaceful environment, as well as courses in personal growth, spiritual practice, and healing. They claim to welcome more than 14,000 visitors every year.

Self-development movements, such as Scientology, say they offer converts the opportunity to achieve true happiness, boost career success, improve their intelligence, and develop self-confidence. Many government and business organizations have paid for management courses run by these movements to train and motivate their employees. Anticult and countercult groups challenge the claims made about the alleged benefits of participating in NRMs.

DEBATE

Should NRMs be allowed to recruit on university campuses? What about freedom of speech? Who decides?

The Children of God/The Family

Christian and Missionary Alliance Church minister David Brandt Berg (1919–1994) started working with hippies in California in the late 1960s. He founded an Evangelical Christian community called Teens for Christ, subsequently known as the Children of God (COG), and reorganized in 1978 to become The Family.

Berg became known as Dad, Moses, or Mo, and he communicated with his followers through "Mo letters," often with comic-strip illustrations. COG members believed that Berg was a prophet who would play a key role at the end of the world. They also applied the Law of Love ("Thou shalt love thy neighbor as thyself," Matthew 22:39) to sexual relationships, thereby permitting sex between consenting adults regardless of whether or not they were married.

COG has attracted a great deal of controversy due to the young age of converts, abuses of power by authoritarian community leaders, the movement's secrecy, and their founder's widely publicized interest in sex. In 1972 concerned parents set up an organization called FREECOG (Free Our Sons and Daughters from the Children of God) to help parents "rescue," and in some cases kidnap, their teenage and young adult children from COG.

Today the movement, which now describes itself as the Fellowship of Independent Missionary Communities, appears to have put many of its past excesses behind it. While Berg's teachings are still considered important, members recognize that his writings are controversial, particularly on sexual matters. These writings have now been reviewed and the more challenging pieces have been destroyed. The Law of Love is still fundamental to the movement, but there are now strict rules on sexual relationships, which may only be between "Family" members. Today the movement's main calling is to tell others about Jesus.

In June 1999 there were more than 10,000 members of The Family. Thirty-seven percent were adults over 21, 8 percent were young adults aged 18 to 21, and 55 percent were children and teenagers under the age of 18. The movement is particularly active in the United States, Britain, and Europe, as well as Latin America and Southeast Asia.

FACT

Actors River and Joaquin Phoenix were COG members as children.

Members of COG in 1978, clad in flowing white robes, march along a busy Miami road. When asked about their destination, they claimed to be "marching to heaven."

VOLUNTARY CONVERSION OR BRAINWASHING?

One of the biggest objections to NRMs is that they allegedly recruit people using deceptive practices and "brainwash" their followers. The term "brainwashing" was coined by British journalist Edward Hunter, following psychologist Robert J. Lifton's investigation into U.S. prisoners of wars' conversion to the Chinese Communist ideology during the Korean War. According to Hunter, this process "[changes] the mind radically so that its owner becomes a living puppet—a human robot....The aim is to create a mechanism in flesh and blood, with new beliefs and new thought processes inserted into a captive body."

In the 1980s, Margaret Singer, a clinical psychologist in Berkeley, California, represented a number of

A member of the Japanese Aum Shinrikyo movement in 1995, with electrodes on his head. This battery-powered headgear was apparently used for "brainwashing and indoctrination."

former NRM members and the families of NRM followers in court, arguing that these groups had used brainwashing or mind control to remove the free will of their members. The Unification Church, Scientology, COG, and ISKCON have all been accused of using mind control techniques to recruit and manipulate their followers.

Although the brainwashing theory provides a convenient explanation for how ordinary people could be persuaded to engage in extraordinary behavior, it has now been discredited. In practice, "mind control" could simply boil down to NRM recruiters being less than honest about who they are, or about the amount of dedication and/or money that their movement requires from members. Recruits have freedom of choice, but might have made a different decision had they had all the facts at the beginning. Many NRMs are criticized for being secretive about their true nature. For instance, the Unification Church has a number of "front organizations," companies (such as Paragon Press, *The Washington Times*, and the Little Angels of Korea dance troupe) that do not appear to be associated with the Unification Church. It has also practiced "heavenly deception"—on the basis that lying was permissible if it was for the good of the church—for instance, to raise funds and attract new recruits.

While it is true that many NRMs' recruitment techniques are highly effective, they are not irresistible. Research has repeatedly shown that most people are perfectly capable of rejecting movements if they wish. This suggests that the decision to join depends on the characteristics of the group and of the individual involved. It should also be noted that high-pressure persuasion techniques and social influence are not unique to NRMs. Such methods are also frequently used in advertising and politics.

VIEWPOINTS

"Most people are recruited into cults, sects, or groups, and my organization would never agree that they 'join.' This is done by deceitful practices and promises which put pressure upon the victim."
Audrey Chaytor, chairperson of Family Action Information and Rescue (FAIR), an anticult movement

"One person's brainwashing is another person's devout or deeply felt belief... what is deceptive to one person is someone else's truth."
Forest Montgomery, National Association of Evangelicals

DEBATE

Are the persuasion techniques used by NRMs any different from those used in advertising?

FACT

The Children of God formerly practiced "Flirty Fishing" [Jesus said: "I will make you fishers of men" in Matthew 4:19], in which women lured men into the movement using sex as bait. This later developed into paid prostitution. The practice was stopped in 1987 as a precaution against HIV.

The recruitment process

It is difficult to generalize about recruitment methods. For instance, New Age movements such as Wicca do not set out to recruit new members, whereas spreading the word and converting new followers are central activities for the missionary Unification Church.

Leading academics suggest that NRM recruitment consists of the following stages:

1. First contact: A chance meeting in a public place with a clean-cut, attractive recruiter. Churches, campuses, and Internet chat rooms are sometimes infiltrated. A potential recruit might be invited for a meal, or to a meeting, training, or discussion group, without being told that it is a meeting of a particular movement.

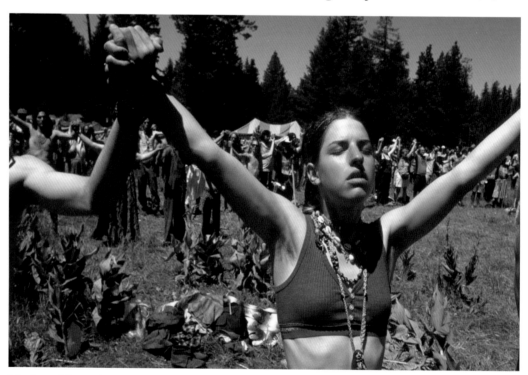

Members of the Rainbow Family, seen here at their annual gathering in the Ochoco Forest in Oregon in 1997, seem to experience a sense of group bonding.

2. Relationship building: The potential recruit has dinner with a group of smiling, talkative people—a "family"—and is invited to a weekend workshop.

3. Encapsulating: The recruit attends a workshop in a remote location. Some of the NRM's beliefs are introduced and the recruit is kept absorbed in group activities such as training, singing, chanting, and meditating. Some NRMs have been accused of controlling diet and sleep patterns, and even using hypnosis, to make the recruit more receptive to their beliefs.

4. Bonding: The recruit is encouraged to bond with the group. It is alleged that some movements practice "love bombing" (showering the recruit with affection and approval), and put great pressure on individuals to join.

5. Committing: The recruit is encouraged to stay on as part of the group.

Impact on individuals

The impact of NRMs on their members is as varied as the movements themselves. For instance, if a bank officer starts meditating twice a day, his family and friends are unlikely to notice a huge difference in his beliefs and behavior. If, however, his teenage daughter returns home from a meeting intending to devote her life to following a cult leader, he might interpret her religious zeal as mental illness.

Members report a wide variety of spiritual experiences during conversion, from "hearing voices" to having "out of body experiences." Families of members have seen personality and lifestyle changes, frequently stating that their relative is "not the same person." In some cases, family and friendship ties are broken; relatives notice secretiveness, trancelike states, use of cult jargon, and rejection of education and work.

VIEWPOINT

"...Cults target people who are in transit, literally or emotionally.... Or you could be between relationships, or going from [high] school to [college]—there are all sorts of situations in which people are temporarily vulnerable.... And the cults tell them, God put you here because he wanted you to meet us."
Ursula Mackenzie, formerly editor of the newsletter of FAIR (Family Action Information and Rescue), an anticult movement

DEBATE

Should families feel pleased or concerned that their child has found happiness as an NRM member?

LIFE IN A NEW RELIGIOUS MOVEMENT

VIEWPOINT

"I reckon I'm about the most brilliant man you have ever met. I must be, to have all these people with university degrees following me—obsession is a weak word for it. These people would follow me around the world till I die."
Raymond Armin, founder and leader of the Emin, a British philosophical movement encouraging self-development

Power

Many NRMs have a charismatic leader or guru, almost always male, whose will is often identified with God's. This leader dictates the movement's beliefs and practices and often has absolute authority over its members. Examples include the Reverend Moon (see p. 14), Jim Jones (see p. 30), David Berg (see p. 38) and L. Ron Hubbard (see p. 22). Many controversies have arisen as a result of the abuse of this power, and many gurus have been accused of exploiting the master-disciple relationship.

Lifestyle

Some movements require members to give up their homes and possessions and live in a commune. The Unification Church, ISKCON, and Rajneesh have all developed isolated communities in which many of their followers live. Many movements have their own schools and even universities, such as the Transcendental Meditation movement's Maharishi Vedic Universities and the Brahma Kumaris' World Spiritual University.

Families of NRM members often complain that these groups lead their recruits to withdraw from the outside world. Some evangelizing NRMs, such as the Unification Church and COG, send members to other countries as missionaries. This is viewed by critics as an attempt to cut them off from family and friends.

Members of the Unification Church (known as "Moonies") have lunch at their isolated compound in central Brazil. Local people come to the center every month to learn how to read and write. They also receive free meals—if they are prepared to listen to several hours of sermons.

Different movements require different levels of involvement. For instance, in contrast to the perception that NRMs demand that recruits devote their whole lives to the cause, people might take a short TM course and have no further involvement with the organization or its Hindu origins. Others take a whole series of Scientology courses and continue leading a normal life, in that they neither work for nor live with the movement. While many people might have been classed as members of an NRM in the last few decades, only a tiny number of core members actually live in a center or work full-time for a movement.

Eastern NRMs tend to involve particularly strict discipline and obedience to a teacher. Many of them ask members to give up their previous life and possessions and keep set hours of worship, rising before dawn to practice chanting and meditation for long hours. Movements such as the Brahma Kumaris and ISKCON are vegetarian. They demand that their followers undergo regular fasting and wear specific clothing (white and orange robes, respectively).

VIEWPOINT

"I felt I had found my home at last. I felt completely carefree for the first time in my life and a feeling of great hope for the future, not just for myself but for the whole world."
A young Moonie's account of joining the Unification Church, reported by Eileen Barker, chair, Information Network Focus on Religious Movements (INFORM)

Family relationships

Some NRMs, such as the Brahma Kumaris, demand that their followers become celibate (refrain from sex). Movements including the Unification Church and ISKCON permit sex within marriage, but only to have children. Marriages in the Unification Church and Sahaja Yoga are arranged by leaders, and the Unification Church is famed for its mass marriages.

Other movements, such as Rajneesh (or Osho, as it is now known), did not discourage sexual adventurousness. In the past, COG has even gone so far as to encourage female members to turn to prostitution in order to recruit new members and raise funds. By contrast, the controversial "Great Rite" of ritual sex between high priest and priestess in Wicca is usually symbolic rather than real.

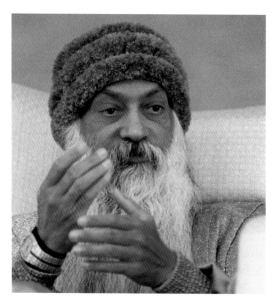

Bhagwan Shree Rajneesh, leader of the Rajneeshis, or "Orange People," seen here at a press conference held in 1985 at Rajneeshpuram, the community he established in Oregon.

There has been widespread criticism that some NRMs confuse sex, religion, and love, and undermine marital relationships. The media has reported numerous scandals concerning sexual abuse and exploitation. Conflicts also sometimes arise between religious duties and the individual's commitment to his or her family. For instance, ISKCON adults were encouraged to become celibate, give up their parental duties, and place their children in ISKCON schools. Problems have also developed when one partner in a marriage has joined an NRM, or when one partner has left a movement while the other remains a member. This "mixed marriage" situation becomes more difficult if the children of such partners remain in the group after one parent has left.

Young ISKCON members throw oil on a sacrificial fire to mark the opening of a new temple complex built by ISKCON in New Delhi, India, in 1998.

Women in NRMs

In some Eastern and Christian traditions, women are seen as having less power and status than men. In certain NRMs based on these traditions, such as the Unification Church and ISKCON, women have a rather subservient, restricted role. For instance, they are unable to take up key positions in the movement and their duties may be limited to looking after the family. Some leaders of NRMs, such as the Children of God and the Branch Davidians, have been criticized for abusing their power by having sex with their female followers.

VIEWPOINT

"Some [cults] exercise their ability to change and outgrow their original cocoon and relate to the human family. The ones that become demonic are the ones that refuse to change."
Rev. Larry Doer, pastor, Lincoln, Nebraska

FACT

In the United States, a Seventh-Day Adventist was refused unemployment insurance when she lost her job in the textile industry. Because of her religion, she was not available for work on Saturday so she could not keep her six-day-a-week job. The woman successfully sued the state of South Carolina, which was forced to compensate her.

Women in groups with a strong emphasis on personal development or that have their roots in pagan tradition often have more power and status than men. For instance, following the death of their male leader, who had stressed the importance of women's spiritual role, nearly all those with spiritual authority in the Brahma Kumari movement belonged to women (Kumari means "unmarried woman"). Other NRMs, such as Wicca, are Goddess religions, which celebrate the power of women. In Wicca, there are twice as many women as men.

Work and money

Some NRM followers, such as Scientologists and TM practitioners, continue to work in their usual jobs. Members of the Unification Church and ISKCON work in small-scale businesses, often selling flowers, plants, candles, books, and other goods door-to-door. Some Scientologists join the church staff and receive free counseling in exchange for what their written contracts describe as "a billion years" of labor.

Bhagwan Shree Rajneesh in one of his forty Rolls Royces, 1984.

Concern has been expressed that some movements demand that followers spend long hours working, fundraising, and worshiping, and get little sleep. NRMs have also been criticized for the contrast between the luxurious lives of some leaders and the harsh living conditions of some members. Bhagwan Rajneesh, for instance, was famous for owning a fleet of forty Rolls Royces, while L. Ron Hubbard and Reverend Moon were estimated to have personal fortunes of hundreds of millions of dollars.

DEBATE

Do parents have the right to refuse lifesaving medical treatment for their child on religious grounds?

Health

Some religious practices, such as meditation or following a vegetarian diet, offer significant health benefits. According to the Maharishi Foundation, more than five hundred studies have been completed on the effects of Transcendental Meditation, finding that those who meditate regularly experience improved mental abilities, health, and social behavior.

However, problems can arise when people get ill but refuse lifesaving drugs or operations because such medical treatments are against their religious beliefs. U.S. courts have ruled that children must have compulsory vaccinations and lifesaving blood transfusions, even when this is against the religious beliefs of their families (for example, if they are Jehovah's Witnesses). Issues also arise when members who have dropped out of mainstream society require medical treatment but do not have the medical insurance required to finance their care.

Jehovah's Witnesses gather at their annual meeting at Villepinte, France. They believe that blood transfusions are against God's will, a belief that has brought them into conflict with medical authorities when they or their family members require hospital treatment.

LEAVING NEW RELIGIOUS MOVEMENTS

Many NRMs have a very high turnover of members. This means that, despite new recruits, the overall membership numbers remain fairly constant. Evidence shows that members are continually leaving all the well-known NRMs of their own free will, even after several years of involvement. For instance, in the 1970s the Unification Church tended to recruit young people quickly, mobilize them as missionaries, and lose a large proportion within a year or so. This has been called the "revolving door syndrome." Much of the negative publicity surrounding NRMs comes from the testimony of former members, often criticized by movements as being embittered. However, research shows that 67 percent of former members who left voluntarily felt wiser for their experience.

People may choose to leave an NRM for many reasons—disillusionment, a crisis of belief, family commitments, or simply a sudden realization that this way of life is no longer for them.

Why do people leave NRMs?

NRMs have a higher dropout rate than mainstream religions, perhaps partly because membership has such a huge impact on members' beliefs, practices, and lifestyle. Some recruits leave after a very short time because the movement did not live up to their expectations. These ex-members often complain that they were recruited by deceptive means. For instance, they might be aware of the movement's belief in loving God but be unaware that this would be expressed in fundraising activities.

Some long-term members choose to leave for personal reasons based on their particular stage in life. For instance, a follower may have given total commitment to an NRM at a fairly young age. Later on, having married and had children, the member may no longer be happy with the commitment demanded by the movement. Some members leave because they fear arranged marriage and other NRM practices.

NRM leaders are often given godlike status, with the result that, if the leader is shown to be corrupt in any way, the follower is likely to become disillusioned with the movement as well as its figurehead. Many former members complain about the dramatic contrast between the comforts enjoyed by leaders and the harsh living conditions experienced by ordinary members. Some allege that leaders are guilty of emotional cruelty and verbal abuse. The death of a leader, and the subsequent power play and confusion, can also lead to members' loss of faith. It is rare for ex-members to report a crisis of belief, although some choose to leave when they find inconsistencies in a movement's teachings. Other members retain their religious convictions even after leaving the movement.

FACT

"The overwhelming proportion of people who get involved in NRMs leave—most short of two years...of their own volition."
Jeffrey K. Hadden. University of Virginia Department of Sociology

VIEWPOINT

"I reflected...and I said, 'Wow, how could a real messiah treat an old lady like that....' I felt I no longer belonged to the Unification Church and I no longer wanted to have anything to do with it. So, I left."
Former member of the Unification Church

VIEWPOINT

"In the first year outside, I cried myself to sleep night after night.... Other kids leave home, but we left our entire lives. Some people can't handle it. They stick together, drag each other down with their stories of what happened to them, get into prostitution, drugs. They get sick. They desperately need help to integrate into society."

Andrew, a former member of COG who grew up in the movement and left at 16.

Many ex-members say that their decision to leave was taken on the spur of the moment in response to a particular incident or realization. Some members literally ran away, escaping in the night from a commune or disappearing while working in the community, often abandoning money and possessions. While most people leave voluntarily, some people are expelled by NRMs for "disruptive behavior" or for failing to raise enough money, and others have been forcibly removed by family and friends.

Why is it so difficult to leave NRMs?

For many members, the movement becomes their family, and they may have close friends and even spouses among other followers. Cult members living in communes have often lost touch with family and friends. The thought of leaving their support network may be a terrifying prospect. Even if they want to leave, they are often dependent on the movement for money and housing. Many followers fear the religious consequences of leaving the movement, and they may find it difficult to break the habit of obedience to a leader.

Many NRMs use specific methods to discourage members from leaving and encourage members to return. These include visits to "health farms" for rest and recuperation, conversations with the guru or leader, and visits from group members. Some NRMs are also reputed to threaten members, both physically and by describing the dreadful religious consequences of leaving the movement.

How do people adjust to life outside?

Former NRM members have been compared to ex-prisoners, mental patients, and members of the armed forces, in the sense that they have been institutionalized. They may find it difficult to reenter mainstream society and adjust to making their own decisions. Many return to their family home as a place of refuge. They are often physically and mentally exhausted and may suffer from anxiety, nightmares, fear, guilt, and feelings of failure.

They also face practical challenges in finding a job or going back to school, finding a place to live, earning money, and repaying debts owed to the movement. Most former NRM members adjust quickly, however, and go on to have "normal" lives, sometimes choosing to continue with certain practices such as meditation or vegetarianism. The biggest problems are usually experienced by those in "mixed marriages," in which a husband or wife has remained in a movement when the spouse has left.

VIEWPOINT

"Even if they re-establish contact with their families—cults often teach that the family is the root of evil—they have ...problems with re-entry. They have no job and have forgotten what it is like to live in the outside world. They may have real problems with hallucinations and obsessive behavior."
Dr. Betty Tylden, consultant psychiatrist

Former members of NRMs face many challenges when they come home, including readjusting to family life.

ANTICULT AND COUNTERCULT MOVEMENTS

There are a number of groups that oppose NRMs, which they usually refer to as "cults." Anticult groups are particularly concerned about the social and psychological effects of NRMs—their impact on the individual, the family, and society. Countercult groups oppose NRMs for religious reasons.

The rise of the anticult movement

In the 1970s there was a huge increase in the number of NRMs, and people were very concerned that movements such as the Children of God and the Unification Church were targeting large numbers of middle-class, well-educated young people. The mass media encouraged parents to believe that NRMs could "brainwash" people and presented NRMs as a major threat to their children. The anticult movement started in response to these fears.

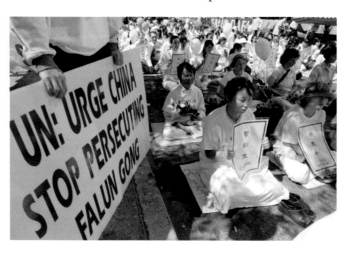

NRMs are sometimes opposed by governments as well as by individuals and groups. Here, demonstrators meditate outside the United Nations building in New York City in 2000 to protest against the Chinese government's banning of the Falun Gong sect.

Who joins anticult groups?

Anticult groups are usually founded by people who have lost contact with a family member because they have joined an NRM. Anticult groups also offer disillusioned ex-NRM members many of the same attractions as the movement they originally belonged to: an inflexible idea of right and wrong and membership in a small community of people whose aim is to "save" others. There have even been organizations for ex-members of NRMs.

The modern anticult movement started with parents' support groups. The Parents Committee to Free Our Sons and Daughters from the Children of God (FREECOG) was founded in 1972. The anticult publicity and high-profile court cases generated by FREECOG led to interest from parents who were anxious about other NRMs, and the movement was expanded to become the Citizens Freedom Foundation (CFF) and later the Cult Awareness Network (CAN).

Several anticult groups developed in the United States and Europe, including the American Family Foundation (AFF), which studies and provides educational resources on psychological manipulation in NRMs; in Britain, Family Action Information and Resource (FAIR), a parents' association concerned about the separation of NRM members from their families; and the Cult Information Centre (CIC), which focuses on the human rights abuses allegedly committed by NRMs.

Other "cult-watching" organizations seek to be impartial. They include academic organizations and "research-oriented groups" which, while tapping the experience of former cult members for firsthand accounts and support for fellow ex-members, try to base their operations on reliable sources of objective information.

FACT

Research shows that the more contact ex-cult members have with an anticult group, either through exit counseling or deprogramming, the more likely they are to interpret their movement in negative terms (i.e., believe they were recruited deceptively, they had been "brainwashed," their leader was insincere, and the group's beliefs were nonsense).

What do anticult groups do?

Anticult groups aim to persuade people not to join NRMs. They give anti-NRM information to the public, the government, and the media, emphasizing the "dangerous" and "cultish" aspects of NRMs. They also try to "save" NRM members by encouraging people to leave and by seeking the intervention of the state through psychiatrists and other mental health professionals. Many anticult groups have also brought court cases against NRMs to help ex-members claim damages or to help parents gain legal custody of their "mentally ill" adult children.

Deprogramming

In the past, some anticult groups tried to kidnap and "deprogram" NRM members. Deprogramming was based on the premise that members had been "brainwashed." The process was justified by the argument that, since no one in his or her right mind would join such a "crazy" movement, members would have to be forcibly returned to rational thinking through "reverse brainwashing." Some experts in "intervention" and "cult counseling" made it their mission to "free" people from NRMs.

Actress Kate Winslet plays an NRM member and actor Harvey Keitel plays the deprogrammer who tries to "rescue" her in the film Holy Smoke.

Governments across the world have since declared deprogramming illegal. Some former NRM members reported that they found the process extremely traumatic, alleging that they were subjected to physical violence, forcible imprisonment, and mental abuse during deprogramming. Many deprogrammed people felt more estranged from their parents as a result. Subsequent scandals led to the collapse of many anticult groups and now voluntary "exit counseling" is generally offered instead.

Countercult movement

The Lutheran Church and the Catholic Church have their own organizations for monitoring and combating cults in a number of countries. These countercult groups target what they believe to be "counterfeit" groups—for instance, those that claim to have a Christian message but whose beliefs and practices are different from the "original" Christian message. Countercult groups aim to correct the "errors" of NRMs and "save souls." They include the Christian Research Institute in the United States and the Reachout Trust in Britain, and they are concerned with all Christian sects, including well-established and accepted movements such as the Mormons and Jehovah's Witnesses.

Anti-anticult groups

For many years the Church of Scientology fought a fierce battle with the Cult Awareness Network (CAN), even publishing a book entitled *CAN: Anatomy of a Hate Group.* Following a court judgment against it in a deprogramming case in 1996, CAN was bankrupted and its assets were bought by a group including Scientologists, which now runs the organization. The new Cult Awareness Network claims to promote freedom of religion and to offer unbiased information about NRMs.

THE FUTURE: PROTECTION, PERSECUTION, OR TOLERANCE?

Whatever interested parties might have to say about NRMs, from their recruitment tactics to their fundraising techniques, very few people ever criticize the central purpose of these movements: spiritual belief.

Mainstream churches have often been reluctant to condemn NRMs because of the need to uphold the religious freedom of belief and practice on which they both depend. For instance, how would people react if Christian parents kidnapped and deprogrammed their daughter in order to prevent her from becoming a Muslim? How would we respond if the state forbade Catholics from taking political jobs because they were deemed to be in the control of a charismatic pope? How would the state distinguish between "genuine" and "cultish" movements? Is there any distinction to be made? The International Association for Religious Freedom has stated its firm opposition to any national legislation imposing restrictions on NRMs that are not also applied to all other religious organizations.

NRMs present us with a seemingly insoluble problem: the right to religious freedom versus the responsibilities of state and family. Many people have called for new laws to restrict the operation of NRMs and "protect" the welfare of the public. However, no one would like to return to the witch-hunts of earlier centuries. Freedom of belief and the protection of religious minorities are central values in modern society. The First Amendment to the Constitution affirms that the state will neither advance nor inhibit religion, establishing rights to freedom of speech, freedom of assembly, freedom of the press, and free exercise of religion; and the European Human Rights Convention recognizes the freedoms to believe, practice, and teach.

Much of society's intolerance toward NRMs stems from modern anticult myths and a history of prejudice against minority religions. People generally agree that religious minorities are entitled to their way of life, providing it does not interfere with the lifestyle of others. However, religious tolerance comes under strain when a movement is considered potentially harmful to society or to infringe on the rights of others, raising questions about national security, family values, the administration of justice, and child welfare. Most governments in North America and Western Europe now agree that existing criminal and civil laws are sufficient, and NRMs tend to be tolerated, unless it can be shown that they are engaged in demonstrably harmful or unlawful activities.

Two Russian members of the Aum Shinrikyo movement stand trial in 2001 for planning to carry out bomb attacks in Japanese cities. They hoped to force the Japanese authorities to free their leader. Three other members of the sect received suspended sentences.

GLOSSARY

acupuncture Chinese complementary medicine in which fine needles are inserted into the skin at specific points to treat various disorders.

alchemy the medieval forerunner of chemistry, based on trying to convert "base" metals, such as lead, into gold.

Alexander Technique a system of promoting physical and mental well-being through awareness of body posture, developed by the actor Frederick Mattias Alexander.

Ananda Marga a movement based on traditional meditation, Yoga, and social reform; founded in India in 1955 by Shrii Shrii Anandamurti; also called the "Path of Bliss."

apocalypse the complete final destruction of the world, as described in the Book of Revelation in the Bible.

Aum Shinrikyo (Aleph) (translation: "the Supreme Truth Society") a movement based on Buddhism combined with elements of Yoga and apocalyptic Christianity; founded by Shoko Asahara in 1987. Following the group's sarin gas attack on the Tokyo subway in 1995, which killed 12 people, the group dissociated itself from its founder, establishing a new code of conduct and becoming known as Aleph.

Brahma Kumaris (Raja Yoga, the Brahma Kumaris World Spiritual University) a Hindu-based meditation movement catering mainly to women (Kumari means "unmarried woman"; founded in Pakistan by Dada Lekh Raj in 1937. Members of this movement practice Raja (meaning "royal") Yoga, wear white robes, follow a vegetarian diet, and lead simple, celibate lives.

Branch Davidians a subsect of the Seventh-Day Adventist Church, the group was taken over by David Koresh, born Vernon Howell. He established a community at Mount Carmel, near Waco, Texas, and increased the movement's strong emphasis on impending apocalypse.

Following a siege by the FBI in 1993, eighty members of the cult were tragically killed in a fire at their compound.

Cabalism (Kabbalah, Kabbala, Cabbala, Quabaleh) ancient Jewish tradition of mystical interpretation of the Old Testament.

The Centers Network *see* **EST.**

charisma powerful personal appeal that can inspire devotion, enabling someone to influence or inspire large numbers of people.

charitable status the position occupied by a charity. Many governments grant charities tax exemptions on the basis that they benefit society. Many NRMs seek charitable status so that they can avoid paying taxes.

Children of God (COG, The Family) an apocalyptic Christian movement that used to put particular emphasis on sexual freedom; founded by David Berg in the late 1960s. The group is now more focused on missionary activity and telling people about Jesus.

cosmos the universe.

coven a group of witches who meet regularly.

druidism a movement based on an ancient pagan Celtic religion.

Elan Vital (Divine Light Mission) a movement based on a combination of Sikh and Hindu teachings; founded in 1960. Following the death of his father, who founded Elan Vital, Guru Maharaj Ji (Maharaji) became the movement's figurehead at just eight years old. In 1983 he changed its focus, dropping Eastern practices and transforming it into a spiritual self-development movement.

The Emin (The Eminent Way, Emin University of Life, Faculty of Color) a self-development movement based on philosophical research; founded in Britain by Raymond Armin in 1972. It draws on New Age interests including astrology and the use of color for healing.

enlightenment the attainment of spiritual insight.

EST (The Forum, The Centers Network) founded in 1973 by Werner Erhard, Erhard Seminars Training is an education program that aims to empower people to transform their lives, become more effective in relationships and at work, and improve their communication skills. EST has now been replaced by The Forum, which is organized by The Centers Network.

Eternal Flame Foundation a Christian-based movement whose followers believe Jesus spoke of physical immortality, which the movement believes is dormant within the cellular structure of the human body.

evangelist a person who seeks to convert others to the Christian faith, especially by public preaching.

The Family *see* **Children of God.**

Freemasons a secret fraternal order, organized as a network of groups or "lodges." Freemasonry is based on Christian mysticism. Masons emphasize the importance of God, "the Great Architect," and brotherly love, by means of ritualistic ceremonies.

guru a spiritual teacher, often playing an important role in many Eastern movements.

Hare Krishna *see* **ISKCON.**

Heaven's Gate founded by Marshall Herff Applewhite, this group's beliefs were based on New Age, Theosophy, and science-fiction ideas. When the Hale-Bopp comet approached Earth in 1997, they believed an alien spacecraft was coming to collect them and helped each other to commit suicide.

homeopathy a system of complementary medicine in which disease is treated by taking minute doses of natural substances that in a healthy person would produce symptoms of disease.

Human Potential Movement a personal development movement, often based on a combination of psychotherapy and sales techniques.

ideology a system of belief.

Insight a self-development movement that organizes Insight Seminars, which promise to help people communicate better and lead more fulfilled lives; founded in 1978 by John-Roger Hinkins.

International Church of Christ (ICOC) an evangelical Christian church that takes the name of the city it is in, for instance, the Boston Church of Christ or the Los Angeles Church of Christ. ICOC specifically targets university and college students.

International Fortean Society a movement with an interest in UFOs and the unexplained.

ISKCON (Hare Krishna movement, Krishna Consciousness) the International Society for Krishna Consciousness has its roots in Hinduism and aims to spread Krishna Consciousness throughout the world. Devotees can be seen in major cities, dressed in orange robes and spreading the word by chanting "Hare Krishna." It was founded in the United States in 1966 by Prabhupada.

Jehovah's Witnesses a Christian sect that has very different doctrines from mainstream Christianity and puts particular emphasis on impending apocalypse and the return of Christ. It was founded by Charles Taze Russell in the 1800s.

Jesus Army (Jesus Fellowship Church) a Christian-based movement that has grown to several hundred members. Followers wear combat uniforms and take part in festivals and marches. It was founded in 1969.

Judeo-Christian based on commonly held Jewish and Christian tradition and belief.

Maharishi Foundation *see* **Transcendental Meditation.**

mainstream religions large, well-established religions, such as Hinduism, Christianity, Judaism, Buddhism, Sikhism, and Islam.

Manson Family followers of Charles Manson.

mantra a word or sound repeated to aid concentration in meditation.

meditate to focus one's mind for a period of time for spiritual or relaxation purposes.

messianic figure a popular, charismatic leader who promises to "save" his followers. The word "messiah" was originally the title given to the king awaited by the Jews, to be sent by God to free them.

Moonies *see* **Unification Church.**

Mormons (Church of Jesus Christ of Latter-Day Saints) a Christian-based sect that has become a major religion very distinct from Christianity, with nearly 11 million members. It was founded in the United States by Joseph Smith in the 1820s. Fleeing religious persecution, Smith's successor, Brigham Young, led followers to what is now Utah and established Salt Lake City.

Nation of Islam established in 1930 by W. D. Fard, it aimed to bring freedom, justice, and equality for African Americans. The group taught that black people were members of the lost tribe of Shabazz, whose religion was Islam. Under the leadership of Fard's disciple, Elijah Poole (Elijah Muhammad), the movement attracted high-profile members such as Muhammed Ali.

Nichiren Shoshu Buddhism (Soka Gakkai) based on Japanese Buddhism, the movement was founded in the 1930s and grew rapidly in Japan and, later, the United States. Practices include daily chanting.

Neuro-Linguistic Programming (NLP) a technique based on studying how people excel in any field, it was developed in the 1970s. NLP aims to teach people to be more successful by examining how people think, communicate, and behave.

Osho *see* **Rajneeshism.**

Pagan someone who follows the ancient religion of their land, often including worship of an Earth Mother goddess and/or several gods.

People's Temple a movement based on Marxism and apocalyptic Christianity. Founder and leader Jim Jones moved his followers from California to Jonestown in Guyana, where a mass murder/suicide took place in 1978.

Raëlians a movement that teaches that the human race was created in their own image by an extraterrestrial race called the Elohim, who have mastered DNA. It was founded in 1973 by Claude Vorilhon, or "Raël." He is seen as the Elohim's messenger who will build them an embassy, allowing them to meet Earth's leaders on a more official basis.

Raja Yoga *see* **Brahma Kumaris.**

Rajneeshism (Osho International, Sannyasins, the Orange People) a movement founded by Bhagwan Shree Rajneesh in 1974. Disciples, or "sannyasins," practice free love and Rajneesh Dynamic Meditation, an active meditation featuring controlled breathing. The guru changed his name from Bhagwan to Osho shortly before his death.

Rosicrucian societies various societies interested in writings of the 1600s telling the story of a Christian named Rosenkreutz who set up a secret fraternity based on magical learnings to reform society.

Sahaja Yoga founded by Mataji Nirmala Devi Sriva in 1970, followers' goal is self-realization and spiritual growth through Sahaja (meaning "spontaneous" or "easy") yoga meditation.

Salvation Army a Christian-based evangelical movement founded by William Booth in 1877. It grew from his mission in the East End of London, where he tried to ease social and spiritual deprivation in the community.

satanism the worship of Satan, sometimes involving a reversal of Christian symbols and practices, with Black Masses and rituals.

Scientology (Dianetics) a self-development movement founded in 1954 by L. Ron Hubbard, based on the "science" of Dianetic therapy.

sect a religious group or faction holding beliefs that differ from accepted tradition; a group that has separated from an established church.

Seventh-Day Adventist Church a Christian-based movement with a strong belief in approaching apocalypse, formed by Ellen G. White in 1860.

spirituality religion or religious belief; concerned with spiritual rather than material things

tai chi Chinese martial art made up of very slow, controlled movements.

theosophy a teaching concerned with ancient religions, philosophies, and sciences, it was founded by Russian mystic Madame Helena Blavatsky and partners in 1875, and was continued by Annie Wood Besant and William Judge. The Theosophical Society promoted the idea that there are "Secret Masters" with mystical knowledge about humankind's relationship with God and the universe.

Transcendental Meditation (TM, Maharishi Foundation) a movement founded by Maharishi Mahesh Yogi, who brought it to the West in 1958. The organization states that TM is a meditation technique, based on Sanskrit mantras, rather than a religion. It aims to help develop the full potential of the individual.

Unification Church ("Moonies") a Christian-based missionary movement whose key text is the *Divine Principle*, which offers a reinterpretation of the Old and New Testaments, combined with some elements of Eastern philosophy. It was founded in Korea in 1954 by Reverend Moon, whom his followers believe to be the Messiah.

voodoo a religion practiced in the Caribbean and in the southern United States, combining elements of Roman Catholic ritual with traditional African rites and characterized by sorcery and spirit possession.

Wicca modern witchcraft.

yoga a Hindu spiritual discipline including breath control, meditation, and the adoption of specific postures, widely practiced for health and relaxation.

Zen Buddhism a fusion of Buddhist and Chinese Taoist beliefs that claims to transmit the essence of Buddhism. Its aim is the direct experience of enlightenment. All ordinary aspects of life, from cooking a meal to driving a car, are seen as a form of meditation. Alan Watts's books on the virtues of Zen Buddhism were widely read in the early 1960s.

INDEX

Numbers in **bold** refer to illustrations.